D0941918

A PORTRAIT OF THE FILM BY MIRA NAIR

BASED ON THE NOVEL BY JHUMPA LAHIRI

26

THE NAM

 Newmarket Press
New York

A Newmarket Pictorial Moviebook

E SAKE

নমসেক

WRITI

সাহিত্ত আর

NG AND FILM

সিনেমা

JHUMPA LAHIRI

THE NAMESAKE BEGAN AS A NOTE TO MYSELF, CASUALLY
JOTTED DOWN AT SOME POINT IN MY TWENTIES,
CONSISTING OF THE PHRASE "A BOY NAMED GOGOL."
For the next five years those four words lay dormant in my notebook,
yielding nothing. The boy named Gogol was literally so: a childhood
friend and neighbor of one of my Calcutta cousins. In the summer of 1992
I went to India and stayed a while with my aunt and uncle and cousin in
the neighborhood of Jadavpur. During that time I often heard the name
Gogol called out from window to window, and from rooftop to rooftop—
my cousin inviting Gogol to play, Gogol's mother summoning him inside
for dinner.

I must have seen young Gogol when he would come over to my cousin's
house, or as the two boys whacked cricket balls on the ground outside, but
what accompanied me back to America at the end of that summer was simply
and persistently a name. I remember thinking that Gogol was an unusual,
somewhat whimsical name for a Bengali boy, but I was also aware that to
people in Calcutta it was unquestioned, understood. Had my cousin's friend
grown up in America, that name, I knew, would most certainly have been
questioned, would not have been understood in the same way.

And so the story took root. I started the first draft in 1997. It was neither
a smooth nor a continuous journey, derailed by doubt, despair, and detours
into two other eventually abandoned novels. I thought I had abandoned
The Namesake, too, but after a long hiatus I finished the book in late 2002.
When it was published, in the autumn of the following year, I was no longer
connected to the novel either emotionally or imaginatively. Though I read
from its pages and talked about it during my book tour, the creative journey
had ended, and I had abandoned Gogol, with better conscience this time,
for good.

By spring 2004 I was working on a new book and pregnant with my
second child. It was then that I met with Mira Nair, and learned that she
wanted a boy named Gogol to be the subject of her next film. I had met Mira
only once before, and though I counted myself among her many admirers,
technically we were all but strangers. But as I sat talking to her in her office,
I felt that we had known each other for years. I sensed that Gogol had
possessed her as he had once possessed me, and I also sensed that she was
about to do something extraordinary. In the course of that conversation
The Namesake passed from my hands to hers, and I stepped back, as a parent

steps back so that a child might discover a piece of the world on his or her own terms.

For the next several months I occupied a parentlike seat along the shore, at once watchful and detached, while Mira swam in open waters. From time to time she would disappear beneath the surface, out of my sight, and then I would get an excited phone call or an e-mail announcing that she had secured the budget, that she had found a distributor, that the screenplay was ready, that casting had begun. I had heard of novels being optioned for cinema and nothing happening for decades, if ever. But less than a year after our initial meeting, not long after my daughter was born, Mira had moved several mountains and was ready to shoot the film.

She had convinced my family to play extras in one scene, and so very early one morning my parents, sister, children, and I all piled into a van bound for Eastchester, New York. It is fairly common in New York City, where I live, to witness a film or television program being made on the streets. But apart from the occasional rubbernecking, I had never visited a movie set. I had certainly never stepped into a trailer and had my hair and face transformed for the camera. More important, I had never understood or appreciated the massive effort and apparatus required for a two-minute scene in a film. There were people to work the camera and lights, people to ferry the props on and off the set, people to bring and adjust and take away costumes, people to mark the floor with tape so that the actors knew where to stand. It was one of the most complicated and exhilarating dances I've ever witnessed. And how strange and wonderful to watch the story I had invented, alone and over the course of so many years, being collectively wrestled with anew.

Ashima and Ashoke get married in Calcutta, surrounded by members of Jhumpa Lahiri's family.

At the center of this creative storm was Mira. Unlike me when I write, she was not locked up in a silent room, jolted from concentration by a mere telephone's ring. She treated the whole day as if it were an enormous party she were hosting, greeting my family with her infectious smile when we arrived, seeing to it that we were comfortable, making sure we'd had enough lunch. She was also present to the details of the set in every way, attuned to each piece of the jigsaw puzzle, at one point calming me down about my (excessive, I thought) hairstyle and instructing the woman in the trailer to flatten my curls. Miraculously, in spite of all this she was utterly focused, in a world of her own making, and making the world of *The Namesake* her own.

PEOPLE TALK ABOUT IMMIGRANTS AS BEING DISPLACED. I prefer the word "transposed," used in music to describe shifting to a different key. That is what happens when a person leaves one homeland for another, and that is what happened as *The Namesake* made its voyage from paper to film. Much like the characters I write about, the story, on-screen, both is and is not itself. Its essence remains, but it inhabits a different realm, and must, like a transposed piece of music, conform to a different set of rules. Books are earthbound entities, ordinary physical objects we hold in our hands and read when we have the time. Film, on the other hand, seems more ethereal, commanding our attention from start to finish, passing before our eyes quite literally like a dream. Movies also occupy a much more public place than novels do. They are publicly created, publicly consumed. But Mira has woven certain strands into the screen that only my family and I can fully appreciate, so that the film remains, for me, a deeply personal experience.

Director Mira Nair, laughing in bridegroom headgear, flanked by actresses Supriya Devi and Tabu, in the wedding scene. Jhumpa's uncle and aunts play in the background.

In real life my nuclear family in America and my extended family in India are separated by about eight thousand miles. But Mira binds us together, in the form of extras embedded in numerous scenes. My daughter, Noor, plays the part of Gogol's sister, Sonia, receiving her annaprasan, when Bengali babies are given their first taste of solid food. Noor's real annaprasan took place just a few weeks after Mira filmed that scene, and mysteriously, maddeningly, our video camera refused to function during the ceremony. As a result, the only footage of Noor's first meal—albeit an ersatz one—is thanks, most serendipitously, to Mira and her sublime cameraman, Fred Elmes.

The detail that touches me most has to do with a few pictures within this picture. Like Ashima's father in *The Namesake*, my mother's father was a painter. When Mira came, in the course of her research, to my parents' home in Rhode Island, she saw some of my grandfather's paintings and asked to borrow them for the set of the film. My grandfather (who happened also to be a great lover of the movies) never had the pleasure of knowing that people around the world would see his watercolors one day. But Mira has done this, too.

Like immigrants who always carry two (or more) places in their hearts, *The Namesake* now lives and breathes in two separate spheres. The changes Mira has introduced are subtle. The timeline has been moved forward slightly, and instead of the anonymous New England town I write about, Mira places the Ganguli family somewhere outside New York. But these are particulars; the song remains the same. Thanks to Mira's passion for a boy named Gogol, I will never think of *The Namesake* as belonging exclusively to me, but as a story we share, one that we were both meant to tell. In my mind this is not a loss, but pure gain. To have someone as devoted and as gifted as Mira reinvent my novel, to watch her guide it safely and exquisitely into the magical arena of the motion picture, has been a humbling and thrilling passage. Together we have arrived at the closest I have felt to artistic collaboration and, most precious of all, an indelible friendship.

JHUMPA LAHIRI
JULY 2006

PHOTO

AS INSPIRA

ছবি তেলার

GRAPHS

TION

প্রেরণা

MIRA NAIR

IF IT WEREN'T FOR PHOTOGRAPHY, I WOULDN'T BE A FILMMAKER. Every film I make is fueled by photographs. Sometimes it is a particular image of a photographer, sometimes it is what I have learned by seeing the world through his or her eyes. Either way, photographs have always helped me crystallize the visual style of the film I'm about to make.

As I prepared to make a film of *The Namesake,* I had an idea for a frame: an image of a dusky Bengali beauty against a Mark Rothko painting in a sleek Madison Avenue space. Then, looking through a book of photographs by Raghubir Singh from the 1980s I came across a startling image of a red T-shirt drying on a flaking Calcutta ironwork railing, decaying Edwardian columns looming in the background. In its rich swath of color amid the layering of centuries, I realized that Rothko was alive and well in modern-day Calcutta. Raghubir's photograph was among the first signs for me that a film of *The Namesake* could be made in an austere photographic style. With the great cinematographer Fred Elmes by my side, we conceived of each scene as a series of wide-angle shots, "democratic frames" within which the actors, not the camera, would move in a choreographed swirl.

The Namesake, for me, was inspired by grief. I had lost a beloved without warning, and as is our custom, we had to bury her the next day, in a bitterly cold field under jet-strewn skies near Newark Airport. This was our Ammy, who had spent her entire life in the red earth of East Africa, now being laid to rest under the icy glare of snow, very far from what she and we, her family, had known as home. In the weeks of mourning that followed, I found myself on a plane reading *The Namesake.* I had bought the novel months before in our local neighborhood bookstore, The Labyrinth, where my family spends many a desultory Sunday afternoon.

"*T-shirt with movie star hanging on the gate of an old mansion, Calcutta, 1986*" by Raghubir Singh

RIGHT
Still from *The Namesake*

Now the book became a comfort, a source of real solace as I tried making sense of the finality of loss. Jhumpa's writing distilled the nature of grief, the loss of a parent in a country that is not fully home, taking readers through a world of crisscrossings achingly familiar to me. *The Namesake* was many of my worlds: the Calcutta I left behind as a teenager, the Cambridge where I went to college, and the New York where I now live. Jhumpa's New York is not the immigrant communities of Little India or Jackson Heights but the New York of lofts, Ivy League bonding, art galleries, political marches, book openings, country weekends in Maine with WASPy friends, a deeply cosmopolitan place with its own images and manners. This was the place I had lived in since 1978; this is the city where I learned how to see.

I had hovered at the edges of the photography world for years, looking at everything from the older masters like André Kertész, Henri Cartier-Bresson, and William Eggleston to the younger New York photographers like Lois Conner, Mitch Epstein, Adam Bartos, and Nan Goldin. Their visual rigor and devotion to the frame trained my eyes. This later became a large part of my enjoyment and practice as a film director.

Yet I never felt the pull to shoot a film in New York until I read Jhumpa's beautiful story. William Thackeray writes in *Vanity Fair,* "The world is a looking glass, and gives back to every man the reflection of his own face." New York was my looking glass and in making *The Namesake,* I could show the world the ease and confidence of the new South Asian cool in the city, how the Desi demi-monde really lived here—a New York that rarely makes its way onto the screen. In her novel Jhumpa managed to tie this world seamlessly, and with incredible specificity and intimacy, to Calcutta. Not only to contemporary Kolkata, but also to the Calcutta of my own youth. I spent

"Untitled, New York #3, 1998"
by Mitch Epstein

LEFT
Still from *The Namesake*

all my summers, from childhood through college, living with a favorite uncle on Cornfield Road, sleeping late, reading, playing cricket in the local maidan, and eventually discovering political street theater there. This was the seed of what later became making films.

It was fitting to return to the city more than thirty years later, in part to pay homage to what I loved about Calcutta. This is a city where culture is worshiped and religion takes a backseat to communism, but also where the goddess Durga presides over every occasion, great and small. The moment I saw Raghu Rai's stunning wide-angle photograph of a laborer carting an adorned Goddess Saraswati across a Calcutta flyover, he gave me the key to include her in *The Namesake*. Thus the goddess of music hovered over Ashoke, Ashima, and Gogol in the film, appearing inexplicably every now and then to bless our tale.

Creative expression is the bread and butter of almost every Bengali, so in Calcutta nearly everybody has a double or triple life. When I was casting *The Namesake*, I attended a symposium of Tagore plays at the Rabindra Bhavan and noticed a particular actor. He turned out to be a successful lawyer who from 9:00 to 6:00 practiced labor law, then performed onstage until midnight. When I asked him how he managed, he said robustly, "It is my oxygen!"

The more I thought about it, the more I felt these two great cities of the world, New York and Calcutta, mirrored each other in specific ways. The massive steel of the Howrah Bridge, like an iconic sash across the Ganges, was echoed in the light grace of the George Washington Bridge across the Hudson River outside my window. I scouted a hospital on Roosevelt Island and felt that it might easily have been a hospital in Calcutta. Ashima could

"Goddess Saraswati being hand-pulled" by Raghu Rai

RIGHT
Still from *The Namesake*

give birth to Gogol here, I thought. She could look out of the window, and in the girders of the Queensboro Bridge, the shake and hum of traffic above and below, would lie the ghost of the Howrah. That is, after all, the state of being of many of us who live between worlds.

Below and above ground, both cities are stitched by rails; the tram tracks of Calcutta, the elevated trains of New York, the subways of both. When alerted by the clang and rattle of the Calcutta tram crossing the main thoroughfare of Chowringhee, I would look across the road to see five planes of faces and cars and bustling buses, eight planes of action crisscrossing each other kaleidoscopically. I could see directly through the tram's windows on Rash Behari Avenue to the shops and the shoppers of Gol Park on the other side, creating wide picture window frames in the manner of Robert Frank's classic photograph. Just like my mornings on the subway platforms of New York City, with passengers across the platform going in opposite directions, then, as each train came in to disgorge and pick up, wiping the slate clean like a screenwipe.

I would shoot these two cities as if they were one. The textures and graffiti, the salaam to both politics and art—these were the gods of both cities. In both you have the frayed and layered posters on the lampposts and walls, scaffoldings of steel in one, of bamboo in the other. Gradually I began to see that the film would be about movement and crossings. The bridges, the trains, the airplanes, the constant comings and goings of an immigrant,

"Veranda, Burdwan House, Calcutta" by Derry Moore

LEFT
Still from *The Namesake*

the neutered spaces of airports and suitcases, would be the threads of the film, uniting its tapestry, covering thirty years in the Ganguli family's life between New York and Calcutta.

All this was in the novel in an understated way, but my film would be a visual realization of that state. The film would begin on a slightly stylized note, following Ashoke Ganguli's trunk gliding through Howrah Station on a coolie's head, the focus remaining on the suitcase as it made its journey into the train carrying Ashoke into his future in America. In Derry Moore's elegiac portrait of the young princess of Burdwan standing in her wrought-iron balcony in late evening light, I saw the longing and stillness of his bride, Ashima, who stepped into her husband's American-made shoes, leaving her web of family and friends behind her, irrevocably changing her life.

When shooting the scene in Kennedy Airport of the last time Ashima sees Ashoke alive, I was guided by the master Garry Winogrand's photographs in his book *Arrivals and Departures* to find secrets in the reflecting floors of airports, where human beings stand in endless queues linked in anonymity, like journeying lemmings. When shooting Tabu as Ashima in Kolkata, I posed her against the gleaming teak doors of Deb Bari on Amherst Street and only months later saw in the frame echoes of Manuel Alvarez Bravo's "The Daydream," in which a young Mexican woman dreams, leaning against a similar stairwell. And sometimes the inspiration was unexpected: in Mitch Epstein's untitled picture made in New York City, the strong graphic of a man on an elevator against a monochromatic red wall once again brought Rothko to mind, and gave me the courage to use a core of strong color in New York suburbia.

The Namesake was also my chance to return the tribute to the great Bengali filmmakers and artists who had nourished me for those twelve

"Minneapolis"
by Garry Winogrand

RIGHT
Still from *The Namesake*

"El Ensueno, 1931"
("The Daydream")
by Manuel Alvarez Bravo

summers and beyond. In 1984, the moment I finished my first documentary, I took the reel under my arm, hauled a projector with the other, and climbed the wooden stairs to Satyajit Ray's home on Bishop Lefroy Road to show him the film. I walked into a scene that could well have been from one of his films: a soiree of great-looking Bengali literati in his study, one reading aloud a brilliant review of his work from *Sight and Sound* fifteen years ago, as the bemused master listened, drawing all the time on a paper resting on his knees.

That was the first of many meetings with the great filmmaker. In distilling the love story between Ashoke and Ashima in *The Namesake,* it was the sweetness and charm of Apu's love for his sudden bride, Aparna, in *Apur Sansar* that I aspired to. One of my great regrets was not knowing the extraordinary Bengali filmmaker Ritwik Ghatak, whose unabashed emotion and Soviet zeal kept me on course through my own shooting in his city. The luminosity of the great Bengali actresses of yore, Supriya Devi (Ashima's grandmother in the film) and Madhabi Mukherjee; the deadly intellectual good looks of the bespectacled Niranjan Ray; the fire in the songs of Nazrul; the confident line and spare color of Jamini Roy—to each of these teachers I bowed in namaskar.

And thus the story possessed me, and the wonderful band of my filmmaking family began clearing the path to make the film happen. Then, as the lady shopkeeper in Kampala proclaims on her storefront sign, "In My Own Way, Ltd.," I set out to make my first Bengali film in America.

MIRA NAIR
KAMPALA, JULY 2006

"Sati Guptoo, Calcutta, 1999"
by Dayanita Singh

RIGHT
Still from *The Namesake*

THE NAM

ESAKE

নমসেক

PHOTOGRAPHS BY

FREDERICK ELMES

NEMAI GHOSH

MILAN MOUDGILL

MIRA NAIR

DAYANITA SINGH

SOONI TARAPOREVALA

HE WAS BORN TWICE IN INDIA, and then a third time, in America. Three lives by thirty. For this he thanks his parents, and their parents, and the parents of their parents. He does not thank God; he openly reveres Marx and quietly refuses religion. But there is one more dead soul he has to thank. He cannot thank the book; the book has perished, as he nearly did, in scattered pieces, in the earliest hours of an October day, in a field 209 kilometers from Calcutta. Instead of thanking God he thanks Gogol, the Russian writer who had saved his life, when Patty enters the waiting room.

"SEEN MUCH OF THIS WORLD?" Ghosh asked Ashoke, untying his shoes and settling himself cross-legged on the berth. He pulled a packet of Dunhill cigarettes from his jacket pocket, offering them around the compartment before lighting one for himself.

"Once to Delhi," Ashoke replied. "And lately once a year to Jamshedpur."

Ghosh extended his arm out the window, flicking the glowing tip of his cigarette into the night. "Not this world," he said, glancing disappointedly about the interior of the train. He tilted his head toward the window. "England. America," he said, as if the nameless villages they passed had been replaced by those countries. "Have you considered going there?"

"My professors mention it from time to time. But I have a family," Ashoke said.

Ghosh frowned. "Already married?"

"No. A mother and father and six siblings. I am the eldest."

"And in a few years you will be married and living in your parents' house," Ghosh speculated.

"I suppose."

Ghosh shook his head. "You are still young. Free," he said, spreading his hands apart for emphasis. "Do yourself a favor. Before it's too late, without thinking too much about it first, pack a pillow and a blanket and see as much of the world as you can. You will not regret it. One day it will be too late."

"My grandfather always says that's what books are for," Ashoke said, using the opportunity to open the volume in his hands. "To travel without moving an inch."

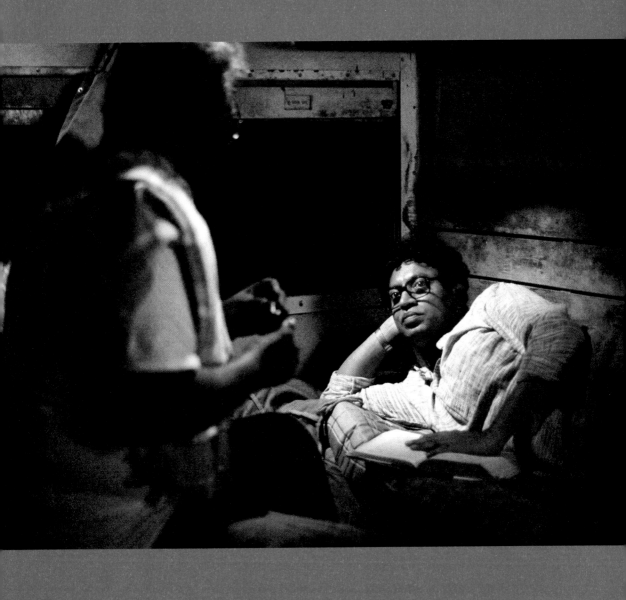

AT EVERY TURNING POINT IN HIS LIFE — at his wedding when he stood behind Ashima, encircling her waist and peering over her shoulder as they poured puffed rice into a fire, or during his first hours in America, seeing a small gray city caked with snow — he has tried but failed to push these images away: the twisted, battered, capsized bogies of the train, his body twisted below it, the terrible crunching sound he had heard but not comprehended, his bones crushed as fine as flour. It is not the memory of pain that haunts him; he has no memory of that. It is the memory of waiting before he was rescued, and the persistent fear, rising up in his throat, that he might not have been rescued at all.

IN THE BEGINNING, for most of the day, he had stared at his bedroom ceiling, at the three beige blades of the fan churning at its center, their edges grimy. He could hear the top edge of a calendar scraping against the wall behind him when the fan was on. If he moved his neck to the right he had a view of a window with a dusty bottle of Dettol on its ledge and, if the shutters were open, the concrete of the wall that surrounded the house, the pale brown geckos that scampered there. He listened to the constant parade of sounds outside, footsteps, bicycle bells, the incessant squawking of crows and of the horns of cycle rickshaws in the lane so narrow that taxis could not fit. He heard the tube well at the corner being pumped into urns. Every evening at dusk he heard a conch shell being blown in the house next door to signal the hour for prayer. He could smell but not see the shimmering green sludge that collected in the open sewer.

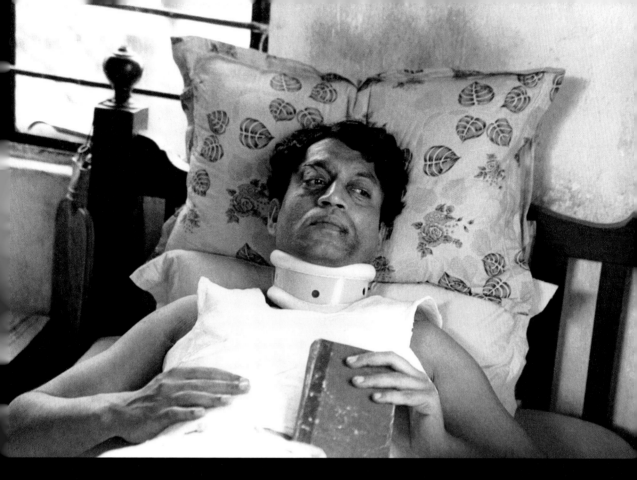

IN THOSE SILENT HOURS, he thought often of Ghosh.
"Pack a pillow and a blanket," he heard Ghosh say. He
remembered the address Ghosh had written on a page of
his diary, somewhere behind the tram depot in Tollygunge.
Now it was the home of a widow, a fatherless son. Each day,
to bolster his spirits, his family reminded him of the future,
the day he would stand unassisted, walk across the room.
It was for this, each day, that his father and mother prayed.
For this that his mother gave up meat on Wednesdays.
But as the months passed, Ashoke began to envision another
sort of future. He imagined not only walking, but walking
away, as far as he could from the place in which he was born
and in which he had nearly died.

1977

AND SO, OBEDIENTLY BUT WITHOUT EXPECTATION,
she had untangled and rebraided her hair, wiped away the
kohl that had smudged below her eyes, patted some Cuticura
powder from a velvet puff onto her skin. The sheer parrot
green sari she pleated and tucked into her petticoat had been
laid out for her on the bed by her mother. Before entering the
sitting room, Ashima had paused in the corridor. She could
hear her mother saying, "She is fond of cooking, and she can
knit extremely well. Within a week she finished this cardigan
I am wearing."

Ashima smiled, amused by her mother's salesmanship;
it had taken her the better part of a year to finish the
cardigan, and still her mother had had to do the sleeves.
Glancing at the floor where visitors customarily removed
their slippers, she noticed, beside two sets of chappals,
a pair of men's shoes that were not like any she'd ever seen
on the streets and trams and buses of Calcutta, or even in
the windows of Bata. They were brown shoes with black
heels and off-white laces and stitching. There was a band
of lentil-sized holes embossed on either side of each shoe,
and at the tips was a pretty pattern pricked into the leather
as if with a needle. Looking more closely, she saw the
shoemaker's name written on the insides, in gold lettering
that had all but faded: something and sons, it said. She saw
the size, eight and a half, and the initials U.S.A. And as
her mother continued to sing her praises, Ashima, unable
to resist a sudden and overwhelming urge, stepped into
the shoes at her feet. Lingering sweat from the owner's feet
mingled with hers, causing her heart to race; it was the
closest thing she had ever experienced to the touch of a man.
The leather was creased, heavy, and still warm. On the left
shoe she had noticed that one of the crisscrossing laces had
missed a hole, and this oversight set her at ease.

OFFERINGS ARE MADE to pictures of their grandparents and his father, rice poured into a pyre that they are forbidden by the management of the hotel to ignite. He thinks of his parents, strangers until this moment, two people who had not spoken until after they were actually wed. Suddenly, sitting next to Moushumi, he realizes what it means, and he is astonished by his parents' courage, the obedience that must have been involved in doing such a thing.

ASHIMA NEVER THINKS OF HER HUSBAND'S NAME
when she thinks of her husband, even though she knows
perfectly well what it is. She has adopted his surname but
refuses, for propriety's sake, to utter his first. It's not the type
of thing Bengali wives do. Like a kiss or caress in a Hindi
movie, a husband's name is something intimate and
therefore unspoken, cleverly patched over. And so, instead
of saying Ashoke's name, she utters the interrogative that
has come to replace it, which translates roughly as "Are you
listening to me?"

FOR BEING A FOREIGNER, Ashima is beginning to realize, is a sort of lifelong pregnancy—a perpetual wait, a constant burden, a continuous feeling out of sorts. It is an ongoing responsibility, a parenthesis in what had once been ordinary life, only to discover that that previous life has vanished, replaced by something more complicated and demanding. Like pregnancy, being a foreigner, Ashima believes, is something that elicits the same curiosity from strangers, the same combination of pity and respect.

IT IS THE FIRST TIME IN HER LIFE she has slept alone, surrounded by strangers; all her life she has slept either in a room with her parents, or with Ashoke at her side. She wishes the curtains were open, so that she could talk to the American women. Perhaps one of them has given birth before, can tell her what to expect. But she has gathered that Americans, in spite of their public declarations of affection, in spite of their miniskirts and bikinis, in spite of their hand-holding on the street and lying on top of each other on the Cambridge Common, prefer their privacy.

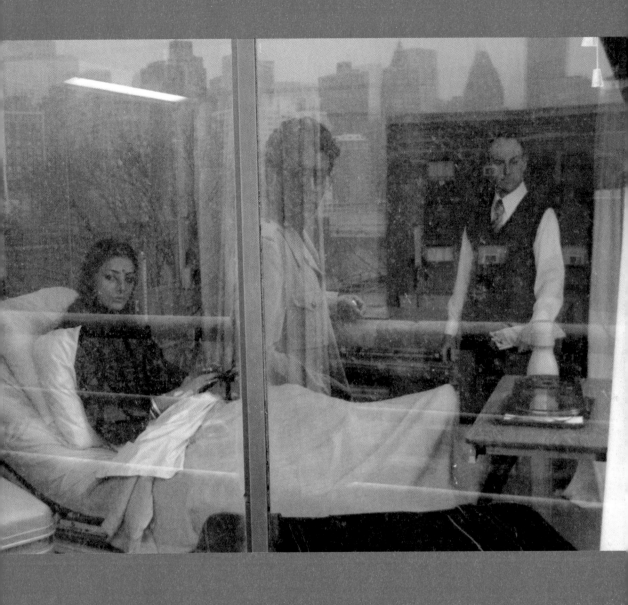

SHE CALCULATES the Indian time on her hands. The tip of her thumb strikes each rung of the brown ladders etched onto the backs of her fingers, then stops at the middle of the third: it is nine and a half hours ahead in Calcutta, already evening, half past eight. In the kitchen of her parents' flat on Amherst Street, at this very moment, a servant is pouring after-dinner tea into steaming glasses, arranging Marie biscuits on a tray. Her mother, very soon to be a grandmother, is standing at the mirror of her dressing table, untangling waist-length hair, still more black than gray, with her fingers. Her father hunches over his slanted ink-stained table by the window, sketching, smoking, listening to the Voice of America.

"WILL YOU REMEMBER THIS DAY, GOGOL?" his father had asked, turning back to look at him, his hands pressed like earmuffs to either side of his head.

"How long do I have to remember it?"

Over the rise and fall of the wind, he could hear his father's laughter. He was standing there, waiting for Gogol to catch up, putting out a hand as Gogol drew near.

"Try to remember it always," he said once Gogol had reached him, leading him slowly across the breakwater, to where his mother and Sonia stood waiting. "Remember that you and I made this journey, that we went together to a place where there was nowhere left to go."

1995

THERE ARE ENDLESS NAMES Gogol and Sonia must remember to say, not aunt this and uncle that but terms far more specific: *mashi* and *pishi*, *mama* and *maima*, *kaku* and *jethu*, to signify whether they are related on their mother's or father's side, by marriage or by blood. Ashima, now Monu, weeps with relief, and Ashoke, now Mithu, kisses his brothers on both cheeks, holds their heads in his hands. Gogol and Sonia know these people, but they do not feel close to them as their parents do. Within minutes, before their eyes Ashoke and Ashima slip into bolder, less complicated versions of themselves, their voices louder, their smiles wider, revealing a confidence Gogol and Sonia never see on Pemberton Road. "I'm scared, Goggles," Sonia whispers to her brother in English, seeking his hand and refusing to let go.

WITHIN THREE MONTHS Sonia has read each of her Laura
Ingalls Wilder books a dozen times. Gogol occasionally opens
up one of his textbooks, bloated from the heat. Though
he's brought his sneakers with him, hoping to keep up with
cross-country training, it is impossible, on these cracked,
congested, chock-a-block streets, to run. The one day he tries,
Uma Maima, watching from the rooftop, sends a servant to
follow him so that Gogol doesn't get lost.

THEY ARE UNACCUSTOMED, after all these months, to being just the four of them. For a few days, in Agra, which is as foreign to Ashima and Ashoke as it is to Gogol and Sonia, they are tourists, staying at a hotel with a swimming pool, sipping bottled water, eating in restaurants with forks and spoons, paying by credit card. Ashima and Ashoke speak in broken Hindi, and when young boys approach to sell postcards or marble trinkets, Gogol and Sonia are forced to say, "English, please."

For two days they wander around the marble mausoleum that glows gray and yellow and pink and orange depending on the light. They admire its perfect symmetry and pose for photographs beneath the minarets from which tourists used to leap to their deaths. "I want a picture here, just the two of us," Ashima says to Ashoke as they wander around the massive plinth, and so under the blinding Agra sun, over-looking the dried-up Yamuna, Ashoke teaches Gogol how to use the Nikon, how to focus and advance the film. A tour guide tells them that after the Taj was completed, each of the builders, twenty-two thousand men, had his thumbs cut off so that the structure could never be built again. That night in the hotel Sonia wakes up screaming that her own thumbs are missing. "It's just legend," her parents tell her. But the idea of it haunts Gogol as well. No other building he's seen has affected him so powerfully.

THE RATLIFFS OWN THE MOON THAT FLOATS OVER
THE LAKE, and the sun and the clouds. It is a place that has
been good to them, as much a part of them as a member
of the family. The idea of returning year after year to a single
place appeals to Gogol deeply. Yet he cannot picture his
family occupying a house like this, playing board games
on rainy afternoons, watching shooting stars at night, all
their relatives gathered neatly on a small strip of sand. It is
an impulse his parents have never felt, this need to be so
far from things. They would have felt lonely in this setting,
remarking that they were the only Indians.

NOW IT IS THREE IN THE AFTERNOON, the sun's strength already draining from the sky. It is the sort of day that seems to end minutes after it begins, defeating Ashima's intentions to spend it fruitfully, the inevitability of nightfall distracting her. The sort of day when Ashima craves her dinner by five. It's one of the things she's always hated about life here: these chilly, abbreviated days of early winter, darkness descending mere hours after noon. She expects nothing of days such as this, simply waits for them to end. She is resigned to warming dinner for herself in a little while, changing into her nightgown, switching on the electric blanket on her bed. She takes a sip of her tea, now stone cold. The petunias in her window box, planted Memorial Day weekend, the last time Gogol and Sonia were home together, have withered to shuddering brown stalks that she's been meaning, for weeks, to root from the soil. Ashoke will do it, she thinks to herself, and when the phone rings, and her husband says hello, this is the first thing she tells him. She hears noises in the background, people speaking. "Are you watching television?" she asks him.

"I'm in the hospital," he tells her.

"I'm sorry, mrs....Ganguli, is it?"

She listens to something about a heart attack, that it had been massive, that all attempts to revive him had failed. Did she wish to have any of her husband's organs donated? she is asked. And then, is there anyone in the Cleveland area to identify and claim the body? Instead of answering, Ashima hangs up the phone as the woman is still speaking, pressing down the receiver as hard as she can into the cradle, keeping her hand there for a full minute, as if to smother the words she's just heard. She stares at her empty teacup, and then at the kettle on the stove, which she'd had to turn off in order to hear her husband's voice just a few hours ago. She begins to shiver violently, the house instantly feeling twenty degrees colder. She pulls her sari tightly around her shoulders, like a shawl. She gets up and walks systematically through the rooms of the house, turning on all the light switches, turning on the lamppost on the lawn and the floodlight over the garage, as if she and Ashoke are expecting company. She returns to the kitchen and stares at the pile of cards on the table, in the red envelopes it had pleased her so much to buy, most of them ready to be dropped in the mailbox. Her husband's name is on all of them. She opens her address book, suddenly unable to remember her son's phone number, a thing she can normally dial in her sleep. There is no answer at his office or his apartment and so she tries the number she has written down for Maxine. It's listed, along with other numbers, under *G,* both for *Ganguli* and for *Gogol.*"

HE RINSES HIS FACE and looks at himself in the mirror. Apart from a day's growth on his face, he looks exactly the same. He remembers when his paternal grandfather died, sometime in the seventies, remembers his mother screaming when she walked in on his father, who was shaving off all his hair with a disposable razor. In the process his scalp had bled in numerous places, and for weeks he had worn a cap to work to hide the scabs.

"Stop it, you're hurting yourself," his mother had said. His father had shut the door, and locked it, and emerged shrunken and bald. Years later Gogol had learned the significance, that it was a Bengali son's duty to shave his head in the wake of a parent's death. But at the time Gogol was too young to understand; when the bathroom door opened he had laughed at the sight of his hairless, grief-stricken father, and Sonia, just a baby, had cried.

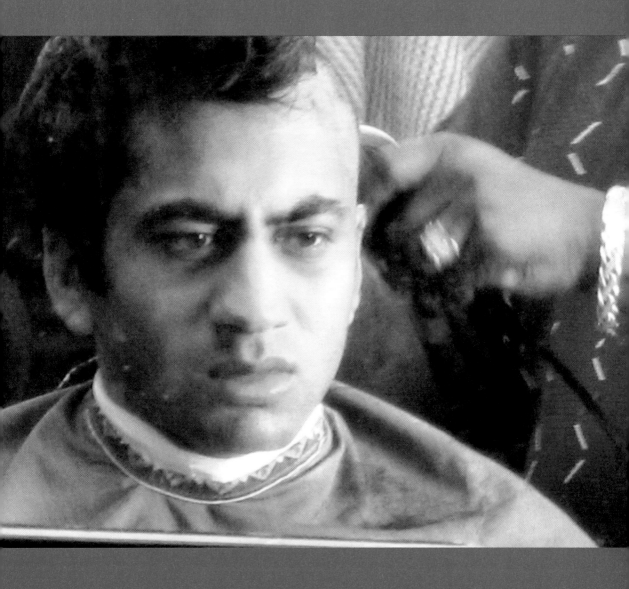

"I'M SO SORRY," he hears her say to his mother, aware that his father's death does not affect Maxine in the least. "You guys can't stay with your mother forever," Maxine says when they are alone for a moment after the ceremony, upstairs in his room, sitting side by side on the edge of the bed. "You know that."

She says it gently, puts her hand to his cheek. He stares at her, takes her hand and puts it back on her lap.

"I miss you, Nikhil."

He nods.

"What about New Year's Eve?" she says.

"What about it?"

"Do you still want to try to go up to New Hampshire?" For they had talked of this, going away together, just the two of them, Maxine picking him up after Christmas, staying at the lake house. Maxine was going to teach him how to ski.

"I don't think so."

"It might do you good," she says, tilting her head to one side. She glances around the room. "To get away from all this."

"I don't want to get away."

FRIENDS SUGGEST SHE GO TO INDIA, see her brother and her cousins for a while. But for the first time in her life, Ashima has no desire to escape to Calcutta, not now. She refuses to be so far from the place where her husband made his life, the country in which he died. "Now I know why he went to Cleveland," she tells people, refusing, even in death, to utter her husband's name. "He was teaching me how to live alone."

2004

"SEVEN THOUSAND THIRTY-FIVE," he announces.

"Not bad, Mr. Ganguli."

"I'd say we've made a killing, Mrs. Ganguli."

Only she is not Mrs. Ganguli. Moushumi has kept her last name. She doesn't adopt Ganguli, not even with a hyphen. Her own last name, Mazoomdar, is already a mouthful. With a hyphenated surname, she would no longer fit into the window of a business envelope. Besides, by now she has begun to publish under Moushumi Mazoomdar, the name printed at the top of footnoted articles on French feminist theory in a number of prestigious academic journals that always manage to give Gogol a paper cut when he tries to read them. Though he hasn't admitted this to her, he'd hoped, the day they'd filled out the application for their marriage license, that she might consider otherwise, as a tribute to his father if nothing else. But the thought of changing her name to Ganguli has never crossed Moushumi's mind. When relatives from India continue to address letters and cards to "Mrs. Moushumi Ganguli," she will shake her head and sigh.

SHE WONDERS IF SHE IS THE ONLY WOMAN in her family ever to have betrayed her husband, to have been unfaithful. This is what upsets her most to admit: that the affair causes her to feel strangely at peace, the complication of it calming her, structuring her day.

ASHIMA HAS DECIDED to spend six months of her life in India, six months in the States. It is a solitary, somewhat premature version of the future she and her husband had planned when he was alive. In Calcutta, Ashima will live with her younger brother, Rana, and his wife, and their two grown, as yet unmarried daughters, in a spacious flat in Salt Lake. There she will have a room, the first in her life intended for her exclusive use. In spring and summer she will return to the Northeast, dividing her time among her son, her daughter, and her close Bengali friends. True to the meaning of her name, she will be without borders, without a home of her own, a resident everywhere and nowhere.

FILM DIRECTOR MIRA NAIR was born in Rourkela, India. From *India Cabaret* to *The Laughing Club of India,* Nair's documentaries paved the way for her remarkable debut feature, *Salaam Bombay!* which was nominated for an Academy Award, a Golden Globe, and a BAFTA for Best Foreign Language film in 1988.

Nair's second film, *Mississippi Masala*, starring Denzel Washington and Sarita Choudhury, was a critical and commercial success. Subsequent films include *The Perez Family*, *Kama Sutra: A Tale of Love*, and *My Own Country*, based on Dr. Abraham Verghese's memoir about a young immigrant doctor dealing with the AIDS epidemic.

In 2000 *Monsoon Wedding* won the Golden Lion at the Venice Film Festival, becoming one of the ten highest-grossing foreign language films of all time. Nair's next film, *Hysterical Blindness*, gave HBO its highest original film ratings in three years. Following the tragic events of September 11, Nair joined a group of eleven renowned filmmakers to tell the true story of a mother's search for her son who did not return home on that fateful day.

In 2003, Mira Nair founded an annual filmmakers' laboratory, Maisha, dedicated to the support of visionary screenwriters and directors in East Africa and South Asia. That same year she directed *Vanity Fair* for Focus Features, starring Reese Witherspoon. She also served as the mentor in film for the prestigious Rolex Protégé Arts Initiative, helping to guide young artists in critical stages of their development.

Nair's company, Mirabai Films, is currently producing a series of four films to raise awareness of the AIDS epidemic in India.

Nair's forthcoming films include *Gangsta, MD*, an African-American adaptation of the Indian comedy *Munnabhai MBBS,* and a feature-length documentary on the Beatles in India.

Nair lives in New York City and Kampala, Uganda, with her husband and son.

JHUMPA LAHIRI was born in 1967 in London, England, and was raised in Rhode Island. She received a B.A. in English Literature from Barnard College, an M.A. in English, an M.A. in Creative Writing, an M.A. in Comparative Studies in Literature and the Arts, and a Ph.D. in Renaissance Studies from Boston University. In 2002 she was awarded a Guggenheim fellowship.

Her first book, *Interpreter of Maladies,* a collection of stories, was published as a Mariner original paperback in June 1999 to overwhelming acclaim. It went on to win the 2000 Pulitzer Prize for Fiction, the PEN/ Hemingway Award, and the American Academy of Arts & Letters Addison M. Metcalf Award. *Interpreter of Maladies* was a *Los Angeles Times* Book Award finalist, and was named Best Debut of the Year by *The New Yorker. The Namesake,* a *New York Times* bestseller, was named a Best Book of the Year by *The New York Times*, *USA Today*, *Entertainment Weekly*, *Newsday*, and the *San Jose Mercury News*. It was named *New York* magazine's Book of the Year. There are over one million copies in print of each of Jhumpa Lahiri's books.

Lahiri currently lives in Brooklyn with her husband and two children.

FREDERICK ELMES is best known for his work with the critically acclaimed filmmakers Ang Lee and David Lynch. For his work on David Lynch's seminal film *Blue Velvet,* Elmes received numerous awards, including the National Society of Film Critics Award for Best Cinematography. His subsequent work on *Wild at Heart,* winner of the Cannes Film Festival Palme D'Or, brought Elmes his first Independent Spirit Award. His multifilm collaboration with Lee began with *The Ice Storm* and includes the Civil War drama *Ride with the Devil,* the innovative short *The Chosen* from the BMW Internet film series, and *The Hulk.*

Elmes has also worked on films by other cutting-edge directors such as Jim Jarmusch's *Coffee and Cigarettes, Night on Earth,* and *Ten Minutes Older;* Tim Hunter's *River's Edge* and *Saint of Fort Washington;* Norman René's *Reckless;* Barry Hersey's *The Empty Mirror;* and Todd Solondz's *Storytelling,* which was a selection for Un Certain Regard at the Cannes Film Festival. More recently Elmes photographed Bill Condon's *Kinsey.*

After studying photography at the Rochester Institute of Technology, Elmes pursued graduate film studies at New York University. The offer of a fellowship at the American Film Institute brought him to Los Angeles in 1971, where he began his long-term collaboration with David Lynch. While at the AFI, Elmes photographed Lynch's cult classic *Eraserhead,* as well as director John Cassavetes's *The Killing of a Chinese Bookie* and *Opening Night.*

Elmes also has been the director of photography on films for television, commercials, and music videos. He's worked extensively in Europe, where his work is highly regarded. In 2000, Elmes was honored for his body of work with David Lynch at the Camera Image Festival in Poland.

NEMAI GHOSH is well regarded for his photographs of Satyajit Ray at work and in his more private moments, and for his stills from Ray's films. Ghosh exhibited at Cannes in 1991, at London in 1992, and several times at Calcutta, Bombay, and Delhi, including the National Gallery of Modern Art, New Delhi. In 1991 he published a selection of his Ray collection, *Satyajit Ray at 70: Photographs by Nemai Ghosh with a Preface by Henri Cartier-Bresson.* In 2005 he published *Satyajit Ray: A Vision of Cinema* (text by Andrew Robinson and illustrations by Satyajit Ray).

Ghosh began his artistic career as an actor and brings to his photography a strong subjective slant, the dramatic moments representing his own reading of situations. Drawing on his memories and associations as an actor, Ghosh composes his shots to underscore the dramatic elements he finds inherent in a scene.

His passion for theater led to a second collection of photographs that forms a pictorial history of theater in Calcutta over the last four decades. He concentrates on the experimental theater groups of the city and its neighborhoods—more than a hundred of them active at any given time—with a repertoire that features a whole range of classical and modern dramaturgy from all over the world as well as original, indigenous works. The photographs capture the distinctive individualities of renowned directors, actors, and actresses in performance as well as in directorial presence.

MILAN MOUDGILL is a graphic designer based in New Delhi, where he runs a design consultancy called Design Em. His first film as a stills photographer was Mira Nair's *Monsoon Wedding*. Thereafter he photographed the Indian schedule of *Vanity Fair* and *The Namesake*.

Milan is a regular contributor to magazines in India as a travel photographer and writer. He is currently working on a photography book, *Kailash-Manasarovar, A Journey to the Center of the Universe*. This project explores a mountain and lake in remote west Tibet that is the site of holy pilgrimage for Hindus, Buddhists, Jains, and Bons, believed by them to be at the center of the universe.

Milan shares a small flat in India's capital with his wife, Mitali.

DAYANITA SINGH is perhaps best known for her portraits of India's urban middle- and upper-class families. These images of people working, celebrating, or resting at home show Indian life without embellishment. She explores another side of India—the place that she belongs to and understands. Her recent work has concentrated on another form of portraiture, of places rather than people. These photographs are taken in a diverse range of interior spaces: from the ballroom of an 18th-century palace to the humbler surroundings of a private home, or from museums, libraries, and seminaries to the specially constructed wedding "stages" of traditional marriage ceremonies.

Dayanita Singh lives and works in Delhi and London. Her work has been exhibited widely both in India and abroad. Recent solo exhibitions include *Chairs*, Isabella Stewart Gardner Museum, Boston (2005); *Privacy*, Hamburger Banhof Museum for Contemporary Art, Berlin (2003); *I am as I am*, Ikon Gallery, Birmingham (2001);

Mona Darling, Venezia Immagine, Venice (1999); *Dayanita Singh and Manisha Parekh, Studio Guenzani*, Milan (1999); and *Dayanita Singh, Family Portraits, Nature Morte*, New Delhi (1998).

Her photographs were also included in Century City at Tate Modern in Spring 2001.

SOONI TARAPOREVALA has had photographs exhibited in India, the United States, France, and Britain.

In 1986 she wrote her first screenplay, *Salaam Bombay!*, for director/producer Mira Nair. *Salaam Bombay!* won 25 awards worldwide, was nominated for an Oscar, and earned Taraporevala the Lillian Gish Award from Women in Film. Her second screenplay, *Mississippi Masala*, also for Mira Nair, won the Osella award for Best Screenplay at the 1991 Venice Film Festival.

Her other produced writing credits include the films *Such a Long Journey*, based on the novel by Rohinton Mistry and directed by Sturla Gunnarsson, which earned Taraporevala a Genie nomination from the Academy of Canadian Cinema and Television; *My Own Country*, based on the book by Dr. Abraham Verghese and directed by Mira Nair for Showtime television, which earned her a Shine nomination; and the film *Dr. Babasaheb Ambedkar*, directed by Dr. Jabbar Patel for the Government of India and the National Film Development Corporation of India.

In 2000 she published a book of her photographs, *PARSIS: The Zoroastrians of India; A Photographic Journey*. A labor of love for over 20 years, the book, a critical and popular success, was out of print within six months. A new edition was published by Overlook Press (NY) and Duckworth (UK) in 2004 and is still in print.

She adapted Jhumpa Lahiri's novel *The Namesake* for Mira Nair.

She lives in Bombay with her husband.

PHOTO
CREDITS
নেমসেক

GRATEFUL ACKNOWLEDGMENT IS MADE TO THE FOLLOWING
PHOTOGRAPHERS FOR PERMISSION TO REPRINT THEIR PHOTOGRAPHS:

P. 12: "T-shirt with movie star hanging on the gate of an old mansion, Calcutta, 1986," copyright © 1988 Raghubir Singh/Succession Raghubir Singh.

P. 15: "Untitled, New York #3, 1998," by Mitch Epstein, copyright © Black River Productions. Ltd./Mitch Epstein.

P. 16: "Goddess Saraswati being hand-pulled," copyright © Raghu Rai.

P. 19: "Veranda, Burdwan House, Calcutta," copyright © Derry Moore.

P. 20: "Minneapolis," by Garry Winogrand, copyright © The Estate of Garry Winogrand, courtesy of Fraenkel Gallery, San Francisco.

P. 23: "El Ensueno, 1931" ("The Daydream"), by Manuel Alvarez Bravo, copyright © Estate of Manuel Alvarez Bravo, courtesy of Colette Urbajtel & The Witkin Gallery, Inc.

P. 24: "Sati Guptoo, Calcutta 1999," copyright © Dayanita Singh.

To Prabhuddo Dasgupta for the photograph on page 138. Copyright © Prabhuddo Dasgupta.

To Fred Elmes for photographs on pages 14, 21, 38–39, 41, 45, 48–49, 59 (2 photos), 60, 63, 64–65, 68 (2 photos), 70–71, 72, 75, 84–85, 98, 101 (2 photos), 102–3, 104–5, 106, 109, 110–11, 112–13, 114, 123 (top photo), 128–29, 130–31, 132. Copyright © Frederick Elmes.

To Marion Ettlinger for photograph on page 139. Copyright © Marion Ettlinger.

To Nemai Ghosh for photographs on pages 7, 13, 43, 54, 56–57, 67, 87. Copyright © Nemai Ghosh.

To Milan Moudgill for photographs on the cover and pages 18, 32, 35, 46 (2 photos), 51 (3 photos), 52, 53, 55, 76–77, 78 (2 photos), 82 (2 photos), 94, 95, 116–17, 119, 123 (bottom photo), 124 (2 photos), 127, 135, 136–37. Copyright © Milan Moudgill.

To Mira Nair for photographs on pages 17, 22, 25, 28–29, 30–31, 36 (3 photos), 44, 88–89, 91, 92–93, 96, 97. Copyright © Mira Nair.

To Dayanita Singh for photographs on pages 24, 42, 69, 80, 81, 86. Copyright © Dayanita Singh.

To Sooni Taraporevala for photographs on pages 8 and 120–21. Copyright © Sooni Taraporevala.

Fox Searchlight Pictures

Entertainment Farm

UTV Motion Pictures Present

A Mirabai Films
& Cine Mosaic Production

A Mira Nair Film

THE NAMESAKE
নেমসেক

STARRING	Kal Penn
	Tabu
	Irrfan Khan
	Jacinda Barrett
	Zuleikha Robinson
	Brooke Smith
	Sahira Nair
CASTING BY	Cindy Tolan, CSA
MUSIC BY	Nitin Sawhney
COSTUME DESIGNER	Arjun Bhasin
CO-PRODUCER	Lori Keith Douglas
CO-PRODUCERS	Yukie Kito
	Zarina Screwvala
EDITOR	Allyson C. Johnson
PRODUCTION DESIGNER	Stephanie Carroll
DIRECTOR OF PHOTOGRAPHY	Frederick Elmes, ASC
EXECUTIVE PRODUCERS	Yasushi Kotani
	Taizo Son
	Ronnie Screwvala
PRODUCED BY	Lydia Dean Pilcher
	Mira Nair
BASED ON THE NOVEL BY	Jhumpa Lahiri
SCREENPLAY BY	Sooni Taraporevala
DIRECTED BY	Mira Nair

MIRA NAIR WOULD LIKE TO ACKNOWLEDGE THE FOLLOWING PEOPLE:

For my filmmaking family: Sooni Taraporevala, Stephanie Carroll, Arjun Bhasin, Fred Elmes, Allyson Johnson, Nitin Sawhney, Robyn Aronstam, Dinaz Stafford, Cindy Tolan— each of you took me further. For my brave actors: Tabu, Irrfan, Kal, Jacinda, Zuleikha, Sahira. With salaams to Deborah Baker Ghosh, for her guidance as a chronicler of my filmmaking journey. Thanks also to my untiring sistahs at Mirabai Films, Ami Boghani and Claire Scoville, for their dedication to detail. A salute to Divya Thakur and the priests at Design Temple for their title design and Bengali calligraphy. Thanks to Peter Rice, Claudia Lewis, Ronnie Screwvala, and Yukie Kito—who believed in this film from the beginning. To Bart Walker, for being my eternal angel in America. Special salaams to my dear friend Lydia Pilcher, for making this book, and the film, come to life.

Produced by Newmarket Press: Esther Margolis, President and Publisher; Frank DeMaio, Production Director; Keith Hollaman, Executive Editor; Linda Carbone, Editor; Paul Sugarman, Digital Supervisor.